SOMEONE SHOULD MAKE THAT!

DRUNKEN IDEAS THAT COULD CHANGE THE WORLD

LoveBook®

Copyright © 2018 LoveBook® LLC
Cover and Internal Design © 2018 LoveBook® LLC
Design & Illustration by Lydia Hillary
Editing by William Bliesath
Contributions by Jared Smith
First Edition

All rights reserved.

Published by Neuron Publishing
www.neuronpublishing.com
www.LoveBookOnline.com

SOMEONE SHOULD MAKE THAT!

DRUNKEN IDEAS THAT COULD CHANGE THE WORLD

Drunken Ideas that Could Change the World is a testament to dreamers and inventors the world over. Straight from the minds of real drunk people, these illustrated product ideas will have you laughing and cringing at the same time. Are you brave enough to see these dreams turn into reality?

This is a book for creatives of all skills and ages (but maybe not too young). Inspire them to design! Or just inspire them to drink.

CONTENTS

1. APPLIANCES

Ambien Light	12
Dribble Drabble	14
Dude Where's My Beer?	16
Face Timer	18
Gasturbator	20
Global Cooler	22
Go-sters	24
Hammered Heads	26
Hydronator	28
Refrigerhater	30
Remasculator	32
Roller Coasters	34
Shower Beer	36
Toilet Chair	38
Urinc Umbrella	40
Wall Punch	42

CONTENTS

2. APPS

Alarmer	46
Clean-Ex	48
Clickskrieger	50
Drunken Riddler	52
Ex-Test	54
Last Call	56
NetPicks	58
Pukepourri	60

3. GASTRO

Dehumidifryer	64
Liquid Discourage	66
Mac & Cheese Tacos	68
Meximaker	70

CONTENTS

4. SOCIAL

Drink Tank	74
Law'n Order	76
Merkintile Exchange	78
Piggle Wiggle	80
Winnebagel	82

5. WEARABLES

Armer	86
Chameleon Pants	88
Drunk Tag	90
Exclamation Pants	92
Funbrella	94
Ghillie Blanket	96
Lit Bit	98
Tank Shoes	100
Vacuumnito	102

1.
APPLIANCES

AMBIEN LIGHT
(am · bee · en · lite)

Tired of being tired but still not getting any sleep? The Ambien Light is at least one solution for your sleep woes! Featuring full spectrum UV bulbs of pure white light (10,000+ lumens) and smooth medication misting action, the Ambien Light will put you under in no time. You'll wake up rested, refreshed, and ready to go again!

The Ambien Light is perfect for insomniacs, light sleepers, and people who gag when they take pills.

DRIBBLE DRABBLE

(dri · bull · dra · bull)

Pissed about having your social life ruined by drunken bedwetting? With the Dribble Drabble, you can save both yourself and your bedmate the wet embarrassment, and sleep soundly knowing that you'll wake up completely dry! Strap the Dribble Drabble on with its patent pending "This Ain't Comin Off" harness and apply the cup to your private area. With airtight suction and reusable disposal containers, the Dribble Drabble could change your life!

Perfect for the occasional (or chronic) bedwetter, excessively lazy people, and those who choose to wait until marriage.

DUDE WHERE'S MY BEER?

(dewd · wares · mie · beeyr)

Upset with repeatedly losing track of your drinks at social gatherings? Try Dude Where's My Beer, the revolutionary new device that allows you to track the location of your drink at all times! With its' state-of-the-art GPS technology, plus any modern smartphone, Dude Where's My Beer is the foolproof way to ensure you consume the entire drink before getting another one.

Dude Where's My Beer is fantastic for active drunks, forgetful folks, and penny pinchers.

FACE TIMER
(faze · tie · mer)

Have kids? A wife? A husband? Familiar with the huge glowing orb in the sky? Who wants to see any of them when you're suffering from a night on the town? Greeting the world with a hangover is the worst thing ever. That's where the Face Timer comes in handy. Simply install Face Timer in your home, automate it to your preferences, and watch as it helps prevent you from having to see anyone, or anything, you don't want to see.

Ideal for family drunks, people with agoraphobia, and half-vampires.

GASTURBATOR
(gas · ter · bay · ter)

Tired of straining your wrists trying to shake every last drop out of the gas dispenser? The Gasturbator allows you to get every last penny's worth of gas into your vehicle without the risk of carpal tunnel syndrome. Simply attach the Gasturbator to the shaft of the gas dispenser and let the magic happen!

The Gasturbator also comes complete with girth adjustments, for the meatier diesel pump shafts.

GLOBAL COOLER

(glow · bull · coo · lur)

Worried about your carbon footprint, but still want to roll in your awesome gas hog? With the Global Cooler, you can have your cake and eat it too! The Global Cooler ensures that you don't ruin the environment with your poor choice of vehicle. With NASA-ish bubble technology, just mount the Global Cooler on your vehicle and watch as it prevents burnt fossil fuels from reaching the atmosphere.

The Global Cooler is made for those who are simultaneously ego and eco-conscious.

GO-STER
(go · stur)

Fed up with people leaving water rings on your precious table surfaces? The Go-ster is here to help! With four robotically-controlled arms that can dynamically detect the grip force needed to hold on, it semi-permanently attaches itself to any container. The Go-ster will prevent your guests from ever leaving a mess again.

The Go-ster is particularly useful for anal-retentive party hosts, clean freaks, and parents of any number of children.

HAMMERED HEADS

(ham · erd · heds)

Fatigued from the "crawl" part of the pub crawl? Hammered Heads will lift your exercise burden considerably! With slightly stolen self-driving technology, Hammered Heads will get you to your next drinking destination faster than you can finish your last beer. The creative shark shape will also provide feelings of empowerment and awesomeness.

Hammered Heads are great for office workers, older people, and multiple DUI offenders.

HYDRONATOR
(high · drow · nate · er)

Sick of having to get up and fetch your own water after a long night of tequila shots? Give yourself the break you deserve with the Hydronator! With a self-cleaning tank of purified water, and a convenient pull-down reel dispenser, simply mount the Hydronator near your bed and have all-hours access to the water your body needs.

The Hydronator is manufactured for alcoholics, people with real disabilities, and mutant hamsters.

REFRIGERHATER
(ree · frij · ur · h8r)

Looking to lead a healthier lifestyle? The Refrigerhater is here to help you get started on the right path, and keep you going! Simply turn on the Refrigerhater, load it up with your usual foodstuffs (condiments and beer), and watch as it scans, analyzes, and evaluates your choices. When it's done calculating, the Refrigerhater will give you helpful, slightly judgmental feedback using layperson terminology.

The Refrigerhater is designed for those living alone, health nuts, and people who respond well to stern authority figures.

REMASCULATOR
(ree · mask · you · later)

Have your house plants been looking a little flaccid lately? Unimpressive to your guests? Give your flowery friends that extra boost they need with the Remasculator! Just set the Remasculator to automatic and let it fertilize slowly over time. Your plants will be swoll before you know it.

The Remasculator is intended to remove the embarrassment of limp, wilting, or undersized plants.

ROLLER COASTERS

(rōll · er · coh · sters)

Ever get tired of constantly toting your drinks around while you're mixing at a party? Roller Coasters will lighten your load considerably! Utilizing defense department multi-wheel technology, just attach the drink to your belt or pants and tow your drink along wherever you go.

Roller Coasters were created for social butterflies, those who gesture wildly, and the incurably lazy.

SHOWER BEER
(shau · er · bier)

Do you receive unpleasant stares when cracking your first beer before nine o'clock? Revolutionize your morning drinking with the Shower Beer! Just hop in the shower, give the Shower Beer a few (hundred) pumps, and enjoy your pre-breakfast buzz. If you've cleaned yourself well, then the shower will mask the scent of the beer and no one will ever know that you've been drinking.

The Shower Beer is a perfect fit for high-performing, career oriented drinkers in positions of power.

TOILET CHAIR
(toy · let · chayr)

Don't like the hard, cold sensation of standard ceramic toilets? Do your business in comfort and style with the Toilet Chair! With cushioned seating and reclining capabilities, you'll never have a bad bathroom experience again. The Toilet Chair also comes complete with an extended flushing mechanism that makes the extra courtesy flush easier than ever.

Heated seat and remote flushing options are also available for an additional fee. Purchase for the bathroom reader, slow go-er, or toilet philosopher in your household.

URINE UMBRELLA

(yer · in · um · brella)

Can you not stand cleaning up errant pee all over the bathroom after a party? On the top of the bowl? The side of the toilet? The floor? Even on the walls? The Urine Umbrella will save you a ton of time and energy! With a helpfully large, concave surface, there's no way the animals you call friends will ever miss their mark again.

The Urine Umbrella is essential for frat boys, halfway house residents, and club owners.

WALLPUNCH
(wahl · punsh)

Need an outlet for your drink, drug, or relationship-induced fits of anger? Want something to hit that's not going to result in prosecution or lost deposits? Try WallPunch! With firm, high-quality drywall and built-in mounting (or optional base), the WallPunch is a socially acceptable outlet for your cheap beer-fueled rage! Simply set it up, go to town, and then show friends your handiwork afterwards.

WallPunch is an excellent option for 18-23 year-old males who need a healthy outlet. Subscription-based service also available; get WallPunch delivered every month!

2.
APPS

ALARMER
(al · arm · er)

Ever find yourself in need of a rideshare at the end of a long night of drinking, only to find that your phone battery is totally drained? The completely original Alarmer app is here to help! Alarmer keeps track of your phone's battery level for you by sending periodic notifications and alarms as your battery level diminishes. Once your phone reaches 5% charge, hitting the snooze button again will result in an automatic call to your parents.

Alarmer was created for people who consistently fail to plan their ride home, have old phones with poor battery life, and those who can't be bothered to look after themselves.

CLEAN-EX
(kleen · ecks)

Furious about seeing traces of your ex everywhere, despite your best efforts? Try out the Clean-Ex app! With the mere click of a button, Clean-Ex will delete, block, hide, and otherwise obliterate all traces of your ex from your devices and social media. For a small additional fee, Clean-Ex will also dispatch a cleaning crew to your home to remove all physical traces.

Clean-Ex is superb for eliminating all evidence of a messy breakup without having to relive any of the pain or embarrassment.

CLICKSKRIEGER
(kliks · kree · ger)

Overly proud of your beliefs and want everyone to know? Download the Clickskrieger app! Clickskrieger allows you to wage ideological warfare on your friends, family, and acquaintances across all of your social media platforms at once. Remove any ambiguity about your politics and maybe even convert some filthy non-believers!

Clickskrieger is beyond compare for basement dwellers, bored singles, and future demagogues.

DRUNKEN RIDDLER

(drunk · en · rid · ler)

Have you done things while drunk that you've come to regret in the cold, hard light of sobriety? The Drunken Riddler app is for you! With ground-breaking predictive technology, the Drunken Riddler can reliably determine if it's probable that you'll make a poor choice in the near future. It then locks down your phone functionality, bank access, and social media until you can solve a difficult series of riddles.

The Drunken Riddler is a necessity for frequent partygoers, fraternity or sorority members, and nearly anyone under the age of 25.

EX-TEST
(x · test)

Done with feeling ashamed and humiliated because you broke down and drunk-texted your ex last night? You need Ex-Test! The Ex-Test app allows you to flag certain phone numbers; if you attempt to call or text them, you will be blocked from doing so unless you can answer a series of ten multiple choice questions correctly.

Ex-Test also comes with two additional levels of security questions you can add on an optional basis, as well as banned words and phrases including, "Still love you," "I want you back," "Come over," and "Do you believe in Unicorns?"

LAST CALL
(lahst · coll)

Ever been stuck still trolling for desperate singles at 2 a.m.? Traditional online dating and hookup sites can be a crapshoot even on the best of days. The Last Call app is different! Last Call propels you to action quickly by notifying you about available people near your location remaining at the end of the night.

The urgency of a diminishing timeframe, and the lower standards created by alcohol consumption, combine to create a deluge of responses! Last Call is like meeting someone organically at the bar, but without any of the pressure - or conversation.

NETPICKS
(nēt · piks)

Need something to do while you browse streaming video apps for ages? Download Netpicks! The Netpicks app plays top trending videos for you while you browse and attempt to choose something to watch. Consume content while you're deciding on what content to consume! Netpicks allows you to fill every moment with quality entertainment (cute puppies). Eliminate the downtime from your downtime.

Netpicks is a must have for the helplessly indecisive, ADHD folks, and those who really just wanted to watch kitten videos anyway.

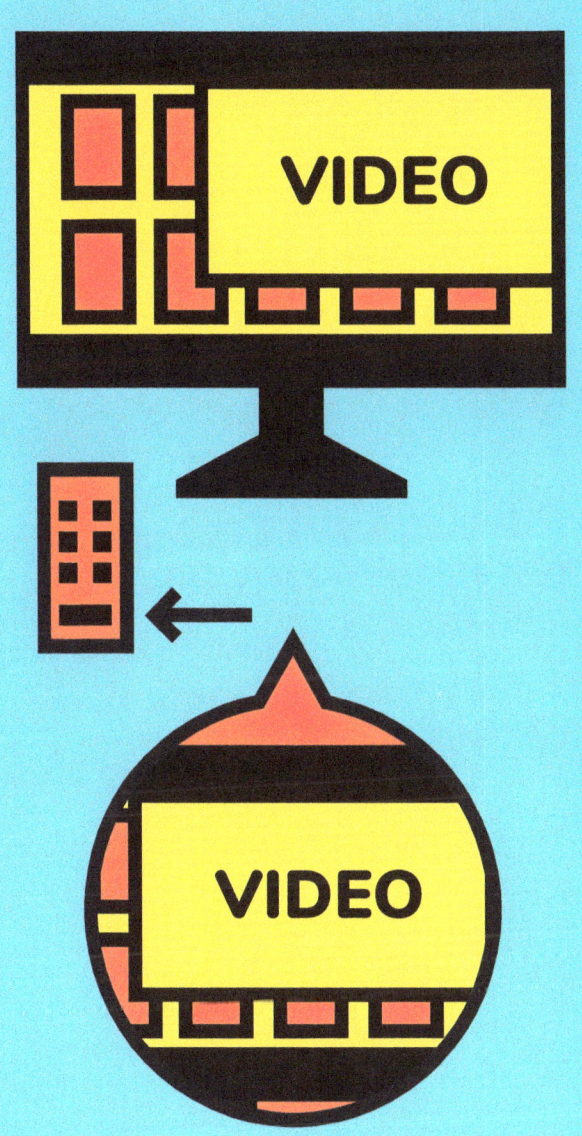

PUKEPOURRI
(pyook · purr · eeey)

Are you one of those people who simply cannot stand even the faintest smell of vomit, not even your own? You need the PukePourri app! Complete with a fragrance-dispensing phone attachment, PukePourri automatically detects the location and nature of the offending source and releases good aromas immediately. The nearly patented perfume comes in five different scent varieties and is guaranteed to mask and eliminate even the most foul of vomitus odors.

PukePourri is useful for preventing vomit chain reactions at large parties or schools.

3.
GASTRO

DEHUMIDI-FRYER

(dee · hyume · ida · fryer)

Hate soggy french fries? Don't we all. Never eat a single soggy french fry again with the Dehumidifryer! Using brand new technology that maintains the heat and crispiness of fried foods without burning or drying them out, the Dehumidifryer is the perfect tool for food pick-up or delivery delays. Simply place the food in the Dehumidifryer, select the appropriate setting, and enjoy your food as though it were just cooked in front of you.

The Dehumidifryer is a fantastic addition to any fast food establishment and food delivery vehicles.

LIQUID DISCOURAGE

(lih · kwid · dis · currage)

Ever needed to sober up fast, quick, and in a big hurry? Try Liquid Discourage! This strangely tasty, not exactly FDA approved elixir brings you back to your senses, no matter how drunk you may be. Simply chug the contents of the bottle and relax as you experience rapid sobriety. Liquid Discourage could save you a lot of money, regret, and jail time.

Formulated for people with a tendency towards drunken tattoo or marriage excursions, and those who are a little too quick to get behind the wheel.

MAC & CHEESE TACOS

(mak · en · chēz · tahcohs)

Can't make the drive to your local taco emporium? Expand your gastronomical repertoire with the Mac & Cheese Taco! This savory blend of greasy American boxed mac and pseudo Mexican corn shell is sure to make your tastebuds dance. Just make the mac (cheap powered "cheese" preferred), add it to a hard tortilla shell, and you're ready to feast.

The Mac & Cheese Taco will really hit the spot if you're drunk, hypoglycemic, or have given up on adulting.

MEXIMAKER
(meks · eee · mayker)

Love burritos, but bored with the usual fillings? Why limit yourself? With the MexiMaker, you no longer have to! Simply load the roller with tortillas, pour in any combination of food you want, and watch as the MexiMaker turns it into a (probably) delicious burrito before your eyes. It's almost too easy!

The MexiMaker is ideal for the adventurous eater, those with no cooking skill, and poor college students.

4.
SOCIAL

DRINK TANK
(dreenk · taynk)

Can't decide whether or not you should text your ex? Or maybe you should buy a drink for that hottie across the bar instead? Call the Drink Tank service! You can get immediate advice from your very own Drink Tank agent. A dedicated operator will then advise you on any social matter for a small fee.

Drink Tank is a great service for the socially awkward, insecure, and friendless.

LAW'N ORDER
(law · n · or · derrr)

Are you looking for a fast, organized, almost militaristic lawn service? Law'n Order is for you! Simply call Law'n Order, explain your situation, and watch as your lawn crew arrives in an intimidating, imitation police vehicle. Not only will you receive top-quality service in a timely manner, but you'll scare your neighbors as well! Law'n Order also offers the option to specify your neighbor's driveway for parking.

Law'n Order is the right choice for suburban landscaping nuts with passive-aggressive tendencies.

MERKINTILE EXCHANGE

(merk · en · tiyal · xchange)

Does it disappoint you that the world of merkin commerce is limited to the internet? Try the Merkintile Exchange service! Simply contact the Merkintile Exchange and a fully-realized merkin market will appear in your location of choice. With Merkintile Exchange, you can build a community of merkin aficionados and meet other like-minded people with one simple call!

The Merkintile Exchange is sublime for merkin fans and the genitally bald the world over.

PIGGLE WIGGLE
(pig · ull · wig · ull)

Is your neighbor's party going way too late, but you can't risk involving the police? You might need Piggle Wiggle! Piggle Wiggle is a service that sends (lightly) armed, uniformed crews to perform crowd control at the location of your choice. Simply call Piggle Wiggle, specify the destination, and watch with glee as a group of police-adjacent bullies clear out the area.

Piggle Wiggle is perfect for households with young children and those with their own aggressive friends who never leave.

WINNEBAGEL
(win · ah · bay · gull)

Tired of Googling all the places that sell bagels in your area? Do you want one simple source where you could acquire all the bagels you want? Try Winnebagel! The Winnebagel service will bring bagels to you anytime, anywhere! With one call, Winnebagel will come to your location with an array of locally sourced bagel choices.

Winnebagel is wonderful for office lunches, parties, and large family gatherings.

5.
WEARABLES

ARMER
(ar · mer)

Have you ever wished there were an easier way to escape from that handsy creep at the bar? Using the Armer, you can be sure to slip out of any sticky situation! Simply attach your Armer to your shirt or jacket and watch as it pops off when tugged. You will never be momentarily paused against your will again!

Armer is useful for approachable women, dashing men, and people who live in rough neighborhoods.

CHAMELEON CLOTHES

(ka · meal · eon · clohs)

Do you get a little clumsy when you drink? Spills (from both inside and outside) happen, and it's rarely convenient to carry a spare dress or pants. That's why Chameleon Clothes are the practical solution to your drunken spilling woes! With a waterproof coating, and heavy-duty, slightly scaly material, Chameleon Clothes can resist even the nastiest spills!

Chameleon Clothes are designed for hard drinkers, accident-prone people, and young children.

DRUNK TAG
(drunnk · taag)

Exhausted by having to track down the drunken wanderers of your party at the end of the night? Get them a Drunk Tag! Complete with identification and tracking technology, you can keep tabs on all your friends, no matter which random gutter they choose to make their bed. Additionally, if you don't feel responsible for collecting this person, you can simply send the location of the Drunk Tag to someone else (or local law enforcement), and have them picked up for you!

The Drunk Tag is convenient for locating almost anyone, but especially after late-night shenanigans.

EXCLAMATION PANTS

(ex · kla · mayshun · pānts)

Looking for a completely unambiguous way of signalling your approval? Exclamation Pants allow you to express your positive feelings in an all-new visual way. No more awkward high fives, hurrahs, or thumbs ups! Just press a button and marvel as the rotator mechanism raises your exclamation point sky-high. Anyone in the area will have no doubt about your endorsement.

Exclamation Pants are tailor-made for office settings, important meetings, and any democratic process.

FUNBRELLA
(fun · brella)

Who says you can't stand in the pouring rain and still have a good time? The Funbrella will protect you, and your drink, from ruination at the hands of harsh elements! With a stabilization harness and built-in drink holder, the Funbrella allows you to enjoy relative safety from the environment while still having your hands free to hold some nachos.

The Funbrella is a must have for those who regularly attend outdoor concerts, sporting events, and backyard barbecues.

GHILLIE BLANKET

(gill · eee · blank · ette)

Just trying to sleep off a long night on someone's lawn in peace? Sick of having the cops called on you? Grab the Ghillie Blanket! Not only will this blanket keep you insulated from nature, but the special forces-looking camouflage material will keep you well hidden from prying eyes. Featuring a lightweight, ergonomic folding design, simply pack the Ghillie Blanket in your pocket or handbag, and be prepared to survive any drunken eventuality.

The Ghillie Blanket is a requirement for wandering drinkers, those who often have their keys taken away, and in the event of a zombie apocalypse.

LITBIT
(liht · biht)

Want to drink and exercise at the same time? Try out the LitBit! LitBit tracks not only your activity, but number of drinks consumed and your BAC as well! With the LitBit you can also share information with your friends and host competitions. Add a productive and competitive edge to your drinking with LitBit.

Designed for healthy drinkers, the relentlessly competitive, and participants in a beer-olympics.

TANK SHOES
(taynk · shoos)

Ever wished for stylish footwear that can strike fear in the hearts of your enemies? A pair of Tank Shoes will have you vanquishing your rivals at top speed! (Or at least causing them terrible discomfort!) With a fully motorized tread system that can carry you quickly across any terrain, and a small but powerful cannon, you'll be terrorizing your neighborhood in no time.

Tank Shoes are best used if you have annoying co-workers, too many frenemies, or belong to a homeowner association.

VACUUMNITO
(vac · yoom · neet · oh)

Offended by getting kicked out of restaurants and bars for harmless vaping? Try the Vacuumnito! With top-of-the-line suction technology, a lightweight body, and clips that attach to everything, the Vacuumnito is the covert solution to your vaping woes! Simply attach the Vacuumnito to your shirt, jacket, or nearby surface and watch as it instantly disposes of all evidence that you've been vaping.

The Vacuumnito also comes complete with a silencer attachment, perfect for undercover office vapers.

www.ingramcontent.com/pod-product-compliance
Lightning Source LLC
Chambersburg PA
CBHW041319110526
44591CB00021B/2839